Stan Grant is a self-identified Indigenous Australian who counts himself among the Wiradjuri, Kamilaroi, Dharrawal and Irish. His identities embrace all and exclude none. He is a multi-award-winning journalist and foreign correspondent who has covered the world's biggest stories of the past three decades. He has worked for the ABC, SBS, CNN, Seven Network and SKY News. Grant published the bestselling *Talking to My Country* (2016), which won the Walkley Book Award, and he also won a Walkley award for his coverage of Indigenous affairs. In 2016 he was appointed to the Referendum Council for Indigenous Recognition.

Writers in the *On Series*

Stan Grant

On Identity

hachette
AUSTRALIA

*Every attempt has been made to locate the copyright holders for
material quoted in this book. Any person or organisation that may
have been overlooked or misattributed may contact the publisher.*

hachette
AUSTRALIA

Published in Australia and New Zealand in 2020
by Hachette Australia
(an imprint of Hachette Australia Pty Limited)
Level 17, 207 Kent Street, Sydney NSW 2000
www.hachette.com.au

First published in 2019 by Melbourne University Publishing

10 9 8 7 6 5 4 3 2 1

A catalogue record for this
book is available from the
NATIONAL
LIBRARY   National Library of Australia
OF AUSTRALIA

ISBN: 978 0 7336 4423 8 (paperback)

Original cover concept by Nada Backovic Design
Text design by Alice Graphics
Typeset by Typeskill
Author photograph by Kathy Luu
Printed and bound in Australia by McPherson's Printing Group

The paper this book is printed on is certified against the
Forest Stewardship Council® Standards. McPherson's Printing
Group holds FSC® chain of custody certification SA-COC-005379.
FSC® promotes environmentally responsible, socially beneficial
and economically viable management of the world's forests.

There are women behind me and I can hear them talking.

'I'm sure I'm related to him,' one says.

'Yes,' replies the other, 'through your grandmother—that was his grandfather's sister.'

It's me they're talking about. I have come here to a place where my father and grandfather were born, a place that I could call 'my country'—a physical space and a state of mind. It is a place far older than what we call Australia, so old that my kinship doesn't run in a straight line but moves in ever-widening circles. I am here to talk about identity—what it is to belong. And it starts with family.

When I turn around they smile and, even though I have never met them, I see faces I have known all my life.

'I'm your Great Aunty Em's granddaughter,' one says.

The other is the granddaughter of my Great Aunty Liz. Elizabeth Knight and Emma Merritt were both my grandfather's sisters.

These women are doing what people I call my own always do, something that is hardwired in us: mapping our family, connecting me to them. Put two or more of us together and it is the first question asked: Where are you from, who are your people? It is genealogy, but it is more than that. It is survival.

We all do this in our own way—people everywhere. It is the family crest, the clan's

tartan, a sepia-tinged photograph, a convict ship's manifest, a long-dead soldier's
pocketbook, the tattooed wrists of the death
camps—tangible proof, because we so need
it. We are not just alive now but alive for all
time. Once a distant ancestor would have
carved the outline of an animal on a wall or
traced her handprint, so that some day someone would see it and know that who was here
mattered. We do this because we know the
truth: 'all things must pass'; time and death
are unstoppable. We live with impermanence,
we will go, all of us, and so we seek to cheat it
all, to tell ourselves that we were here before
and will be here again.

The science that has given us the power
to obliterate humankind has also given us
the gift of eternity. Now we can push back

even beyond shared memory, following our bloodline into all corners of the globe. We have decoded the human genome, a scientific book of Genesis that reveals who begat who until we reach our mythical Adam and Eve. We buy DNA kits that tell us we are never who we think we are—the Italian woman who discovers she is Ashkenazi Jew; the Scotsman surprised that he has long-lost relatives in Kenya; the African-American who is as much Norwegian and Navajo.

There are three billion letters in our genetic code and almost all of them are identical. The scientific truth is 99.9 per cent of our DNA is similar to everyone else. Think about that, all of our difference, all of the things we hold true—or at least we think they are—contained in that fraction of a per cent. What horrors we have committed in that tiny space between us: those wars, slavery based on race, conquest and colonisation. But that tiny space between us has given us such beauty too: art and language and music, new words for God, new ways of explaining our universe. All that brings colour to a grey world.

Michelangelo knew something when he painted the Sistine Chapel. He left a space between those outstretched hands of God and Adam. Before scientists had measured the distance, Michelangelo gave us that space to find ourselves. That space we call our world is the phenomenological world of philosopher Immanuel Kant—we bring into being only what we know, it is through our experience we understand. But the world can also be too much for us. Albert Camus knew this world as the 'absurd'. 'Understanding the world for a man,' the French philosopher and author wrote, 'is reducing it to the human.' Camus wondered of who and of what can we truly say, 'I know that.' I know my heart; I can feel that; it exists. He said, 'This world I can touch, and I likewise judge that it exists. There ends all my knowledge, and the rest is construction.'

And the rest is construction.

We have entered the world of identity— that fraction of DNA, that space between the hands of God and Adam. That space holds the battle for power, our politics or ideology, our faith or our atheism, all our love and hate. In that space we become strangers, even strangers to ourselves. In that space, says Camus, is all of our absurdity, and 'the absurd becomes God … and the inability to understand becomes the existence that illuminates everything.'

In a perfect world I would have no need to write of identity, but the world is not perfect and identity is one of the reasons why. It consumes me. It is the thing I must write about if I am to be free to write about anything else. There is no other way; identity was foisted on me before I could even choose what I wanted to be. There were names for people like me—Aborigine, half-caste, Aboriginal, Indigenous—and many more that I won't repeat here because to do so would only give them power and those names have caused enough damage already. It is enough to know that I am none of those things, even if at times I have had to be all of those things.

I am an invention—a fiction, an historical anomaly stumbled upon, discovered and then denied. The names I have been given have erased whatever it is I could have been, and put in its place what others could see, or more precisely what others were prepared to see. Captain Cook first named my ancestors. He called them 'Indians', then 'natives', and then he decided for legal reasons they didn't exist at all and claimed for the Crown the land their people had lived on for tens of thousands of years.

Since then there have been dozens and dozens of official names for people like me, and our fate was determined by what name fell upon us. One of my great aunts, for example, was called a 'half-caste' and taken from her family to a dormitory where she slept with other girls under a sign that told them to 'think white, act white, be white'. She wore white gloves and a long dress and, with the other pale-skinned Aborigines, was marched into town and back to go to school, and then, one day, would be sent to work for a white family and, if all went well, would find a white man and have ever-whiter children. In her case it didn't work. She found her way back to her family, met a blacker man and had ever-blacker children before she died when she wasn't even forty.

What a failure she must have been to a society that made a fetish of colour. It was government policy to keep Australia white. We even invented a peculiarly Australian mathematics for it: if you took one black woman divided her descendants by three generations of white men all the blackness would disappear. They had a word for it: 'assimilation'—the natives would be 'absorbed' into the Commonwealth. There was an equation for the banned Chinese too: they were told, 'two Wongs don't make a white'.

The worst thing that happened to me was being born what was termed 'black'. It is also the greatest thing to happen to me. The worst is that my fate—at times in history whether someone like me would live or die—could be so arbitrarily decided by others. To be born black meant having always to explain myself, because I wasn't really black at all. If I am the sum of genes, I'm as white as I am black.

But I learned a lesson very early on in life, one that is the most important lesson a person deemed black can learn: whiteness is not a colour. White people—or as writer James Baldwin would have said, people who believe they are white—don't need an identity. They can, if they desire, speak French, German, Italian, and no one will ask them where do they really come from. Being white is a passport to glorious anonymity.

Whiteness historically has meant power. Not that black people cannot have power or that all white people are powerful, but let's agree that whiteness has set the rules of the game. Think about democracy, liberalism, capitalism, fascism and communism. Depending on the eye of the beholder, some of them are wonderful things. Democracy and liberalism are to my mind among the greatest dreams humanity has dreamt, but being deemed not white means you have to work from the outside in. Funny thing is, the closer you get—the more successful, the more powerful—the whiter you become. Years of being a journalist, appearing on television, travelling the world and enjoying all the privileges of comparative wealth means I now have that dubious honour of being told that I'm 'not like the others' or, 'but you're not really one of them'.

I learned the rules of this game as a very young boy. Baldwin said he had spent a lifetime watching white people and outwitting them so that he may survive. It was easy really, for me, when confronted with that question, 'What are you?' Lie. I was lucky I had some strategic cover, just enough of the European to get away with it, but still black enough to know that I could be caught out. How many times I was, for convenience sake, a Maori or a Tahitian, a Hawaiian on occasion—never white, but more acceptable. The alternative in some of the gravel-hard, outback schools I turned up in was to prepare for battle, or run.

I read a book when I was young with a title that was irresistible: *The Autobiography of an Ex-Colored Man*. I remember a line in it:

> I know that I am playing with fire and I feel
> the thrill which accompanies that most fas-
> cinating pastime; and, back of it all, I think
> I find a sort of savage and diabolical desire
> to gather up all the little tragedies of my life,
> and turn them into a practical joke on society.

James Weldon Johnson wrote those words in 1912. He tells the tale of an unnamed, mixed-race man in America—someone black who could so easily pass for white. Indeed, for most of his childhood he believes himself to be white. His life is a struggle between what people see and the 'truth' he seeks to hide. His 'whiteness' is his 'practical joke on society'. In the end, surrounded by tragedy and loss, he considers the middle-class white man he has chosen to be and wonders if he has 'sold his birthright for a mess of pottage'.

Johnson's book captures the existential dilemma of identity: to choose life his anti-hero must deny his black mother and so a part of him dies. He believes he is choosing freedom but its cost is guilt and shame. He spends a lifetime seeing himself in every dark face and turning away. In his America, one drop of black blood is all it takes to be cast out, segregated, mocked or lynched. He escapes his fate, finds love with a white woman who becomes bound to his secret, and together they and their ever-'whiter' children extend their 'practical joke on society'. In truth, he reminds us that no one is free when whiteness and blackness depend on the negation of the other. What is left is a struggle for power, the whip and the white hood to keep order, returned with a simmering vengeance.

What is the practical joke I am asked to perform? To tell the world that I am black, that I am an Aboriginal person. Unlike Johnson's ex-coloured man, it is not my blackness I must cast aside, but my whiteness. On every government form, every school enrolment, every sports team registration form, every medical appointment, there it is, that question that demands just one definitive answer: Are you Aboriginal or Torres Strait Islander? A nation that has never really known what to call someone like me has at times wished us to disappear. Now it wants me to settle the matter: yes or no.

John McCorquodale, the legal historian, counted sixty-seven definitions of being ... I don't even know what to call it now, but let's settle on ... 'Indigenous'. It has been a forensic business, decided on an arbitrary reading of something called 'blood quantum'. What it has been is a quasi-scientific experiment—like measuring skulls—to decide who qualifies to be free. At a time when Australia measured its wealth by the pound, in wool and gold, it counted people in fractions. Some of this nation's greatest minds have been applied to the task: Justices of the High Court, and all of them white. In a series of statements from the bench in the 1980s and 90s, judges tried to define Indigenous identity.

Justice Deane thought: 'By "Australian Aboriginal" I mean, in accordance with what I understand to be the conventional meaning of that term, a person of Aboriginal descent, albeit mixed ...'

Uh-huh.

Or try this from Justice Brennan: 'Membership of the Indigenous people depends on biological descent from the Indigenous people and on mutual recognition of a particular person's membership by that person ...'

Well, that's so much clearer.

Justice Spender introduced a novel idea: If it is 'established that a person is, non-trivially, of Aboriginal descent, then that person is Aboriginal within the ordinary meaning of that word ...'

Easy isn't it. Now, all we have to do is establish what is 'non-trivial' in the ordinary meaning of those words.

To this we have tasked our finest minds: the quixotic quest to strain the biological soup produced by Australia's clandestine history of miscegenation, to separate each ingredient and divine the worth of human beings. It would be hilarious had this not been so harmful. Remember, too, that in many parts of this country for much of our history it was illegal for whites to 'cohabit'—a sly euphemism if ever there was one—with blacks. People like me, like my parents, were evidence of a crime.

I said that being born black is the worst and best thing to happen in my life. Here is the best: love. My family loved with the ferocity of poverty. My family banked their love like the rich bank money. It wasn't the love measured in inheritance, in property, but the love that knew no favour or condition. It was the love that was never counted, but shared. I know that if I am to fall destitute there is a small place on this earth that will always take me in and ask nothing in return. It is a love bigger than Australia because it does not seek to measure or divide us.

That's the problem with identity boxes: they are not big enough to hold love. Every time I have to answer that question, 'Are you Aboriginal or Torres Strait Islander?'—as I was asked to do in the census of 2016—I am required to deny my grandmother. My son is required to tick a box that excludes his mother.

My grandparents, Keith and Ivy, loved each other with an intensity that defied their country and in time likely drove both of them more than a little bit mad. Keith was a young black man who lived by the river in a tent and Ivy was the blonde-haired blue-eyed girl he would whistle at as she walked by. One day she moved in and worlds shook. Australia could not understand this love, so it was banned. It was a love bigger than my grandparents too, and they could never hold on to it. But Ivy stayed for thirty years and had thirteen children.

She had a hard time, Ivy. She was turned away from hospital while giving birth to her first child because it was going to be the wrong colour. Police would stop her in the street and turn over her pram, searching for grog—they suspected she was secretly running to the blacks' camp. She lived in a tin humpy with her kids, until the police came at gunpoint with a bulldozer and ran it to the ground. Two of her children died young. Ivy lived on the margins, always on the outside of town, always an outsider. Ivy was on the wrong side of the colour line in an Australia where those things mattered, even though Ivy was white. In 1940s Australia, blackness was contagious.

Now I can erase my grandmother from my history. With an 'x' scratched on a page, it will be as though she never existed. This woman who bathed me, fed me, who each birthday sent me knotted handkerchiefs stuffed with loose change, gone, removed without a trace. Now my hand is poised on a page and I'm pondering this question: 'Are you Aboriginal or Torres Strait Islander?' One box that, I'm expected to believe, holds all that I am.

In that box all the blurred lines of my confounding, contradictory, complicated family history are dissolved into one definitive statement of being. What life can be reduced to this? My favourite food, my favourite film, my favourite book, how can those things, those hundreds of little choices we make, be contained in this one box? What assumptions that box holds, that I must prefer the didgeridoo over the cello, that dot paintings will hold more beauty than Picasso, that the stories and mysteries of the Dreaming must, for me, possess more profound truths than the rational thought of The Enlightenment. In that box I am being asked to choose when I would rather embrace it all. In that box I am being asked to declare allegiance with many I have never met over a woman without whom I would not be here.

Ivy Sutton is a part of me; her alabaster skin has lightened the hue of my own. Through her I map my DNA on the great human migration across Europe. These are the invisible traces of who I am; the small lives of my count-less ancestors, each a footnote in a history of war and revolution, disaster and disease. On and on, these people—my people—adrift on an endless sea to find each other. A world unstable destabilises us, we are a community of fate, we die at each other's hands, as we are kept alive by the love and kindness of strangers. French poet Arthur Rimbaud is right: 'I is another … I make a stroke with the bow; the symphony begins in the depths.' We are a human symphony, the songs of so many lands. The unknown does not terrify us. The other is within us; it is how we evolve.

The psychologist Alberto Melucci puts it so beautifully: 'We are migrant animals in the labyrinths of the world metropolises; in reality or imagination, we participate in an infinity of worlds.' There is no place on this earth where we cannot be found, no walls that can keep us divided—however we may try. For Ivy, the journey of her ancestors led her to a world so unlikely, to the Kamilaroi of north-western New South Wales, to a man in a tent, to my mother, to me.

If I mark yes on that identity box, then that is who I am; definitively there is no ambiguity. I will have made a choice that colour, race, culture, whatever these things are, they matter to me more than my grandmother. All across Australia people just like me are being asked to deny their family members. Is deny too harsh a word? Betray then? What else are we to call it? If suffering and the impact of racism were the measurements of belonging then Ivy Sutton would have far greater claim than me. But by a quirk of biology, by an accident of DNA, I have what is deemed a 'non-trivial' amount of 'Indigenous' ancestry and that is enough to separate us. By that alone I can claim to be something that my grandmother could never be.

'You can't be a bit and bit. What are you, Noongar or Wadjela?'

In his book *Kayang & Me*, the novelist Kim Scott takes the reader on a journey into his own search for belonging and meaning and reveals something that has long troubled me about identity: how easily it morphs into tyranny. Scott is being asked if he is black or white, he can't be both. It seems to me a cruel question, in its own way as cruel as the police who brutalised my grandparents. It comes with the same assumptions of power: we will tell you who you are and whether you belong; we will determine your identity; you will answer to us. For Scott, it is also an impossible question, because of course he is both Noongar and Wadjela; he is 'a bit and bit'. He describes himself as fair-skinned, raised with little contact with Noongar people. He says he didn't grow up in the bush; there were no stories around the campfire. 'I knew very few members of my extended Aboriginal family,' he writes, 'and they were either ashamed to admit to their Aboriginality or—like my father had perhaps been—too diffident to loudly identify themselves as Aboriginal.'

When Scott learned of his ancestry, his father told him he was 'of Aboriginal descent', It was a softer phrase; more polite somehow than saying bluntly, 'you are an Aborigine'. So when confronted with that question— Noongar or Wadjela?—Scott really has no answer. All he has is politics. He writes that he felt:

> the political imperative about the need to commit, to align oneself with either white or black, and I felt compelled to obey. There didn't seem to be any choice, not if I wished to be among Noongars.

Compelled, commit, obey, align; these are words of identity, not words of love. I have done a word search for love in *Kayang & Me* and it never appears. Things are 'lovely'—he writes of a 'lovely day', a 'lovely spot'—there are even 'loved ones'. But not love. In its place is identity—'identity' is mentioned more than forty times. It confirms what I have come to believe is true: identity—exclusive identity—has no space for love.

It isn't that he doesn't mention love in his other novels, but it always seems to be somehow fleeting, peripheral, love with an asterisk: 'a kind of love', 'a father's love', 'a sort of love', 'love, I suppose'. I look for the spontaneous, crazy, wild, irresponsible, dangerous love of people who love in spite of all good sense and all warnings not to—the love of my grandparents, the love without which I would not be here. What I find in *Kayang & Me* is something more studied, cautious and deliberate. It is more scientific than emotional. It owes less to pheromones and more to physics.

To find himself, Scott must enter a rip in time—what the physicist John Wheeler called a 'wormhole', a shortcut through space. Scott—like me—is where time has deposited him. It is the time that came in the boats.

Time marked the journey—they started on a date and they arrived on a date: 26 January 1788. Time measured the push into tomorrow. Time was progress.

Time is history—that's what Georg Hegel said. To the Prussian philosopher, time was an arc from tyranny to freedom. In the beginning one was free, then some were free, then all were free. It was the quest for the 'absolute spirit', the very end of history. From thesis to antithesis to synthesis. A man cannot step twice into the same river, for he is changed and the river is changed. Indeed it is he who changes the river, and it is the river that changes him. Once time has begun we can never go back.

There is another measurement of time. Not Western time, but the time Indian philosopher Sarvepalli Radhakrishnan calls, 'the

great world rhythm. Vast periods of crea-
tion, maintenance and dissolution follow each
other in endless succession.' Wisdom is not in
the future; it is in the return, the coming and
going, the endless repetition. British anthropologist David Maybury-Lewis says time in
old Australia—the time of my ancestors—was
different entirely, it did not move forward or
return in cycles, but was 'past, present and
future all present in one place'. It is why some
in my family find it so easy to believe that they
see ghosts.

Scott writes ghost stories. In *Kayang &
Me* he talks to his ancestors, patchily recalled
stories of long-lost relatives. He sifts through
a roll call of names and a maze of government
documents. His is a meditation on home, family, truth—whatever that is—and belonging.

Scott knows that identity is a story we tell ourselves, it is a construction—not entirely a work of fiction but selective of its facts. A narrative emerges; it is a narrative of loss and exile, marked by catastrophic events: rape, pillage and massacre.

He is on a rescue mission to free his family from what Scott has called the 'sickly stream of Australian literature'. It is something Scott talks about a lot, and is a recurring theme in all of his writings. He has said that 'writing fiction' is 'sometimes a way to explore, to rethink and possibly to retrieve or create something from between and behind the lines on the page.' It is writing as therapy, it is writing to save a life.

The late psychologist Michael White would have described Scott's story as a process of 're-membering'. White developed something he called 'narrative therapy'. Through our stories, he believed, we are able to reimagine or reinvent ourselves. It is a shadow line we walk between our lives and the memories of the dead. In *Kayang & Me*, it is a line that connects Scott with so many other people who feel a rupture in their lives, a sense of being cut adrift from their true selves.

Philosopher and anthropologist Michael Jackson says, 'life is a road, and in travelling it we both follow the tracks of those who have gone before and leave traces of ourselves …' When Scott chooses the narrative of the road, he is not just telling a story; he is mapping a path for others to follow. In interviews, Scott has said that in revealing oneself the writer can help others to become who they are.

Scott, in grappling with his own place in the world, becomes a type guru of myth, guiding others into that forest where they will find the grail of their inner 'Aboriginal' self.

Writer Samuel Beckett said, 'I have always sensed there is in me an assassinated being.' I am reminded of that when I read the testimony of people we call the 'Stolen Generations'. One after another they speak of 'something missing', feeling like an 'empty shell', or that there is a 'wound that will not heal'. Members of my own family suffered from being separated from their parents, their siblings and communities. It is a pain that I have seen passed down through the generations. It is as though, for them, time sped up just as their world froze. They are forever out of sync.

There are lost seconds they can never recover.
In the words of one survivor:

> We may go home, but we cannot relive
> our childhoods. We may reunite with our
> mothers, fathers, sisters, brothers, aunties,
> uncles, communities, but we cannot relive
> the twenty, thirty, forty years that we spent
> without their love … We can go home to
> ourselves as Aboriginals, but this does not
> erase the attacks on our hearts.

The years spent without love, that is the
great hurt. Love; love beyond any colour.
And where there was no love, they now have
only the search for identity. The philosopher
Hannah Arendt said, 'The greatest injury
which society can and does inflict, is to make
[the pariah] doubt the reality and validity

of his own existence.' There is something worse: it is to make them believe there is no love in the world. In the grief of the Stolen Generations survivors, the loss of love is forever linked to the loss of being Aboriginal.

One man remembers being sent to a foster family, where 'I had no identity. I always knew I was different. During my schooling years I was forever asked what nationality I was, and I'd reply "I don't know".'

As painful as it is, 'I don't know' may be the better answer—the more honest answer—to Scott's question: Noongar or Wadjela?

That question confronts us with the necessity and the impossibility of identity. By answering so affirmatively 'Noongar', Scott gives up a chance to write in that space between us, that space where he could have been neither

Noongar nor Wadjela, or both, or sometimes one and sometimes the other or even one, both and the other at the same time. The endless possibilities were surrendered to certainty. 'Tell them you're a Noongar,' one of his old aunties, Kayang Hazel, says, 'be yourself, Kimmie.' Be yourself, be a Noongar—he is told again and again, he can't be a 'bit and bit'.

Scott finds something heroic in this, and at its best perhaps it is. In writing himself back into a Noongar identity he leaves a trail of breadcrumbs for others lost or stolen to find their way home too. But I can't help feeling it is a little sad. Sad because it isn't love that calls him, but politics. Remember, it was the 'political imperative', he had 'no choice'; if he wanted to belong he had to be a Noongar. But we always get to choose. The real question is what we are prepared to lose. To choose freedom, to choose love, may come at a big cost—it may even cost your life—but to choose politics just to belong, for me, would feel like losing a bit of my soul.

As Scott has chosen he must make it so. He must wrest his 'blackness' from the grip of his 'whiteness'. Everything is reclaimed—language, culture, place, family. For Scott, Indigenous identity is something to be excavated, like an archaeological dig. Like archaeology, the shards of artefacts can only tell us so much of the past. We lay them out in a museum and allow our imaginations to fill in the spaces. Scott becomes a Noongar through an enduring mystical and mythical spirituality and the stories of pain and suffering.

Scott destabilises and unsettles whiteness; he speaks back at it:

> I followed ancient footprints and knelt to drink from waterholes, felt my palms settle in smooth hollows in granite where many, many hands had rested ... my breath entered internal spaces ... as if I was being reshaped from the inside out.

I am captivated by Kim Scott's work, and deeply admire him. He is a powerful writer and I am drawn into deeper and deeper conversation with him, asking ever-harder questions of myself. There were times in my life when I would read him through one eye, studying his words, looking for some reflection of who I might be. But I read him now

with both eyes open and I realise that we are
worlds apart. If I am Aboriginal, then it bares
little resemblance to how Scott imagines it. I
don't find who I am in reclaiming or recre-
ating the past. I didn't grow up apart from
anything. The waterholes and hands of my
ancestors were never distant. That doesn't
make me better than someone else. It makes
me very fortunate and it makes me different
to other people, like Scott.

I have spent most of my life looking into
the eyes of other Indigenous people, searching for that spark of recognition, that gentle
nod that says we are here—we exist. History
had written us out—the pillow of death was
being smoothed for us. If we would exist at
all it would be only in memory. But who can
accept so easily the verdict of history? We

were made to wage war against it, just to exist. Scott's identity is drawn from the memory of those old battlefields; it is an identity precious and unique to him. But I see now that we speak different languages, and that's the point. That's how it should be. Whatever it is to be Indigenous—to be Noongar, or in my case Koori—it is not one thing. The world has asked us different questions.

As a boy I was never forced to choose between being black or white. In any case it would have been ridiculous, because white people lived among us. They were married to us; they had children with us. If there was an 'us', they were part of it. I want to speak to the whiteness within me, not against it: 'I is an other.' The people I grew up with, who I call my own, who were seen as black and had a 'black culture', also went to a Christian church. Christianity was as spiritual as the Dreaming. The Christians in *Kayang & Me* are never black. In me there is no more inner battle to be waged, no peace to be found, no resolution or reconciliation. I would rather dwell in the *mitwelt* —the 'with world'. I prefer the tender indifference of the world, the hope of being without choosing.

But Scott knows too that this question, 'Noongar or Wadjela?', is a terrible one to ask. In *Kayang & Me* he confronts his own choices. He wonders if his own psychological, political and spiritual preoccupations have not 'led my children into a "no-man's land", made them targets from either side of a social schism, a historical, racial fault-line.' He writes, 'Have I stranded them where stress is inevitable while we live among Noongar and Wadjela people in a divided society?'

Identity does not liberate; it binds. To even attempt to speak against identity confirms an identity of its own. It is the head of the Medusa—to look upon identity turns me to stone. Yet, the French offer escape. They have another word that is a counterpoint to identity: *altérité*. It describes the self and the other. This is what I choose to see when I gaze into the mirror, when I look on the faces of my children.

This is what Edouard Glissant has called 'the poetics of relation'. It is possible, he says, 'to be one and multiple at the same time; that you can be yourself and the other; that you can be the same and the different.' Glissant had need only look to his own life. He was a poet and philosopher from Martinique, someone we might see as black. He was descended from slaves and he imagined that journey of his ancestors on boats—Africans bound to the hulls of slave ships. The Africans were set adrift on an ocean between two distant shores. It was a journey into the truly unknown, a voyage into the abyss. Glissant believed he carried within him the dimensions of that abyss. 'And I think,' he said, 'the abyss's dimension is not, contrary to what one might believe, the dimension of Unity, but rather the dimension of Multiplicity.'

Glissant imagined a 'creole garden', not the slave plantation. White cotton is no longer king, but there exists a network of plants supporting and giving life to one another. There is no one root, extending and choking off all around, but a subterranean network of entwined roots, pushing new buds and stems to the surface. The 'creole garden' of people and cultures is a haven, he said, from a world of often-brutal certainty, the dangers of the 'rooted identity'.

Like me, Glissant is an exile. Beyond love, exile is a great gift I received from my parents. We were constantly on the move. We looked at life from the outside. Don't confuse exile with homelessness or rootlessness—exiles carry home within them. Glissant said the exile is on a 'search for the other'. 'Dweller and pilgrim,' he wrote, 'live this same exile. On boats we carried stories, and those stories have passed on through time.' He writes, 'We cry our cry of poetry. Our boats are open, and we sail them for everyone.'

My ancestors were castaways on boats. Away, back in time, people stepped ashore on this continent. Those exiles had made the first open-sea journey in the history of humanity. Two centuries ago my Irish great-great-grandfather John Grant, a young rebel fighting the British, was exiled for life to this new penal colony on the other side of the world. He would never see his home again, but made a new home and a new family here. They were no longer just Irish or just black, but something else, something always becoming, something that cannot be contained, cannot be put in boxes.

The great Irish poet WB Yeats wrote, 'Everything exists. Everything is true and the earth is only a little dust under your feet.' I carry the dust of Ireland on me. It dwells in the love of word and story; stories passed down through time. My great-grandfather was called the 'storyteller'. His mother was a Wiradjuri woman, whose name is lost, and his father the Irishman. He was born in the 1850s before Australia was Australia, before cars and aeroplanes, and he died in 1940, when the world was at war. The old people who remember him tell me he carried with him everywhere the stump of an old carved Wiradjuri ceremonial tree. He would set it up and tell stories of old times, until the fires faded into the night.

These storytellers of exile speak to me. If I am Aboriginal, then read through my eyes they become 'Aboriginal' writers—they help explain my world. Glissant is an 'Aboriginal' writer. He speaks to me of possibilities. I have read many 'Aboriginal' writers: James Joyce, WB Yeats, Czesław Miłosz, Franz Kafka, Albert Camus. Richard Flanagan is an 'Aboriginal' writer; he is a brother to me as sure as anyone who may claim to be Indigenous. He is an exile, too, who writes in what others might see as a distant and cold place, but all the better to see the world. Flanagan taught me that Camus was a Tasmanian writer, because Flanagan was a Tasmanian and he read Camus there and it changed his life.

To Flanagan, 'writing at its best exists beyond morality and politics.' He says,

'Nations and nationalisms may use literature, but writing itself has nothing to do with national anythings.' So it is of identity—identity warriors may use writing but writing has nothing to do with identity anything. Kafka said, 'How can I have anything in common with the Jews, I have nothing in common with myself.' These writers—these 'Aboriginal' writers—these exiles, they are people between, set apart from land or memory. And where land and memory crushes in on them, solely defining them, they push against it.

I read Yeats and Joyce with the old Irishman John Grant looking over my shoulder. He joined his name to the roll call of resistance, those who sacrificed life and liberty for a free Ireland:

From where shall we draw water,
Said Pearce to Connolly,
When all the wells are parched away?
O plain as plain can be
There's nothing but our own red blood
Can make a right Rose Tree.

Yeats wrote those words after the nationalist Easter uprising of 1916. His poem 'The Rose Tree' imagined a conversation between two rebels—Pearce and Connolly—as they ponder how they will breathe life back into their land. Yeats was the great poet of Irish nationalism; he well understood, even empathised, with the pull of the identity of grievance.

The real Patrick Pearse, nationalist and revolutionary, spoke of the 'ghosts of the Irish nation', the ghost of 'whom you must do the thing it asks'. And the big things that ghosts ask, Pearce writes, 'must be appeased whatever the costs'. Nothing but their 'own red blood'. As a reporter, I saw up close the anger in the blood when I covered The Troubles of Northern Ireland—Catholic and Protestant in pitched battle that set Belfast alight to what seemed like a hundred fires.

In Belfast, identity festered between the Shankill and the Falls; two roads—one Protestant, one Catholic—separated by a few hundred metres but entirely foreign countries. Between them a lethal no-man's land. I walked the Falls and summoned my Catholic roots, looking for that old Irishman who is still somewhere in me. But the Falls took me back to somewhere else: to the dirt road between the Three-Ways Aboriginal mission of my childhood and my hometown of Griffith, and how between them stood Australia.

For so many years the identity of resentment held sway over me; an identity dipped in my people's red blood. Yeats walked that line between Catholic nationalist grievance and the dream of an Ireland released from sectarian hate. Yeats, the Irishman, found his own exile in words—he wrote in English to tell a story big enough to speak the stories of the oppressed in the tongue of the oppressor. And he warned of the folly of unquenchable vengeance: 'the man whom sorrow named his friend', who sang his sorrow to sand and stars, and for whom the wind 'changed all he sang to inarticulate moan … forgetting him'.

James Joyce found his Ireland far from his country. In him I see my own journey, living away from Australia for the best part of two decades and in the stories of others trying to make sense of where I had come from, in their voices always hearing the whistle of home. Joyce chose exile in Europe, where he spoke back to his native land. In Joyce's *A Portrait of the Artist as a Young Man*, Davin, the rebel, worships 'the sorrowful legend of Ireland'. He is the idealist, a nationalist who seeks to convince Joyce's hero, Stephen Dedalus, that nation must be put above all else. As Joyce wrote, Davin's nurse had 'taught him Irish and shaped his rude imagination by the broken lights of Irish myth'. Yet Dedalus—Joyce's literary alter ego—knows if he is to write anything he must find freedom; he must shake loose the chains of identity:

Mother is putting my new secondhand clothes in order. She prays now, she says, that I may learn in my own life and away from home and friends what the heart is and what it feels. Amen. So be it. Welcome, O life! I go to encounter for the millionth time the reality of experience and to forge in the smithy of my soul the uncreated conscience of my race.

Camus told me of the folly of resentment, the 'evil secretion ... of prolonged impotence'. Resentment, he wrote, is always 'resentment against oneself'. Camus spoke to me of the world of the exile, 'a world suddenly divested of illusions and lights, man feels an alien, a stranger'. In this world, man seeks unity in nostalgia, even the nostalgia of violence. Man is prey to his truths, he wrote, and if he wants truly to be free, he cannot be a prisoner of any identity. As Camus wrote, he should 'strive to escape the universe of which he is the creator'.

The universe of identity stifles the writer. It destroys the writer's great gift, to be able to speak and be heard beyond one's own. A poet has no identity—John Keats said that, and I say amen to him. Dead at twenty-five, he published barely more than fifty works and yet is revered as perhaps the greatest of the English Romantic poets. To be British is to love Keats. And how he loved his homeland, its smells, its sounds, he drank and ate of it:

O, for a draught of vintage! That hath been
cool'd for a long age in the deep-delved
    earth,
tasting of Flora and the country green …
Ode to a Nightingale

It's an irony that a man who longed to be free of identity should become a symbol of Britishness.

The British see themselves in him, but then so do I. Am I then British? No. Keats' words are not encoded in DNA, they translate across all bloodlines, races or cultures or languages. Not for Keats the straitjacket of identity. He longed for what he called 'negative capability', 'that is when man is capable of being in uncertainties, mysteries, doubts without any irritable reaching after fact and reason'. The writer must experience the world in all its uncertainty.

Keats believed that the true poet 'has no self—it is everything and nothing'. He was the chameleon poet, 'continually filling some other body'. He could be Iago or Imogen and delight in both. In a letter to his friend Richard Woodhouse, Keats said a 'poet is the most unpoetical thing in existence'. Identity was crushing, it was the enemy of the creative, in a room of people, the identity of everyone, he wrote, 'begins so to press upon me that I am in a very little time annihilated'.

Annihilated. The soul-eroding, stultifying, expectations of identity. That demand that you will be this and no other. You will exist only in opposites. Difference will define you. Identity like this can steal the joys of childhood. There comes that day when someone says, 'That's not yours; they aren't your people'. I remember how, as a boy, I would sit, for what seemed like hours, staring at a painting that hung on my great-aunt's wall. It was of a fox hunt— riders in full red regalia, galloping horses, dogs leaping over green hedges. It transported me to some place I had never been, but could imagine as my own. It was so English and eventually I came to understand that I was not English and so, in time, I looked away— for a time away from everything that was not 'mine', not 'Aboriginal'. It is then, and in hundreds of little moments just like that, when, as Wordsworth wrote, the 'shades of the prison-house begin to close upon the growing boy'.

Identity becomes a prison-house. We are locked in with only those who are deemed our own for company. It is the prison house of our own imaginations—these fictions, these stories carefully woven from collective memories, memories that are not even one's own, but we are convinced are more real because of that. Collective memories are the most evocative memories of all. They are handed down with the authority of ancestry and how can we doubt our ancestors? Collective memories are so powerful they must be whispered, all the better at night or around a campfire. We lean in closer; we breathe these stories in until they become fixed. What happened to our ancestors becomes what happened to us. A collective memory soon becomes a collective nervous system.

Japanese writer Haruki Murakami says 'history is collective memories'. In writing, he says, he is 'using my own memory, and I'm using collective memory'. Lest we forget, we are tied to a history of remembrance. The French philosopher Paul Ricœur tells us we must remember; in remembering 'we stop the victims being buried twice'. Our ancestors are rescued from the cold storage of history. See how collective memory takes shape: 'victims', 'loss', 'defeat', 'humiliation'.

Yes, there are heroes too: warriors, fighters. Those who are triumphant get to build monuments to their myths. History is written by the victors. For victims, the myths fester; the indignity burns. The Chechen, the Basque, the Navajo, the Palestinian, the Irish, they all know this. To the victors history is an inventory, a glorious wall of remembrance—names, dates, times, places. For the victim, history is an autopsy, what remains of the dead. How they died—a violent death, an unjust death—comes to matter more than how they lived. Resentment becomes the iron in the blood of the identity of loss.

To French historian Michel de Certeau we create a history of absence. The door to the future is locked and we are trapped in a room where all that is left to us is to arrange the artefacts of our collective memories. This is history as psychoanalysis. We are trapped in a Freudian world of the 'uncanny', where the familiar is strange. In the uncanny we speak with the dead not to study history but to make history. The dead appear in the present as 'ghosts', as 'phantoms'—we are haunted by events we cannot change, but would not want to change because what happened then makes us who we are now.

Around and around we go, in and out of our past that is not past but now, talking to those long gone who are kept alive in us. We breathe them in, until we cannot separate their breath from ours. I say no to this. I say no to breathing someone else's life. What can I possibly say if I cannot breathe? Am I to believe that I am forever on the losing end, my memories will only be the memories of wounds? This narrative of grief distorts our genes—scientists call this epigenetic inheritance. The collective memory chokes off our biology, some genes cannot express themselves; they are stunted. It ends in mental illness, heart disease or cancer. It is the toxic stories we tell ourselves that can kill.

I am with Keats: for a writer there must be no identity. Not just in his case for the freedom to write as man or woman, but for the need to breathe, to live. To write against identity is to choose life—all the more urgent if all around you is death. The Polish Nobel Prize laureate Czesław Miłosz spoke of his 'strange occupation' writing poems in Polish while living in France and America. He was a child of Europe living in the heart of darkness in the twentieth century. He wrote of violence, genocide and silence. He sought to give voice to that silence, to 'write in a dark age,' he said, but 'longing for the kingdom of peace justice'.

He was writing to a future not a past. He was writing against the violence of identity, not to form new identities.

Toni Morrison talks to ghosts in her novels. Her characters have felt the plantation whip and chains and it has made her long to be free—in her words 'to think about how free I can be as an African-American woman writer in my genderised, sexualised, and highly racialised world'. In an old lecture, Morrison once said the 'very serious function of racism is distraction.' This racism, she said, 'keeps you from doing your work. It keeps you explaining, over and over again, your reason for being.'

The distractions, she said, are the constant need to drudge up things—culture, art, memories—just to prove one is worthy. I see it now in the sorry burden of writers who feel the need to reconfigure, reconstruct, reimagine more romantic visions of some lost mystical past. They construct identity just to say to the racist, I exist! It is a Sisyphean task, one without end. Morrison said 'none of this is necessary. There will always be one more thing.'

For Morrison, writing has been the struggle to live free of the white gaze. 'Our lives have no meaning, no depth without the white gaze,' she says, and she writes to ensure the white gaze does not loom over her. Her characters are black, unapologetically black. They arrive fully formed out of a black experience. It is the world she has inhabited; it is her inspiration. She has been accused of being fixated on race, unable or unwilling to write white characters, yet for that to be true we would surely need to accuse Tolstoy of being fixated on Russia. Morrison, like Tolstoy, finds in the particular the universal. It does not make her an identity writer; the opposite is true. The identity writer is always writing back to whiteness, it is whiteness—even attempting to escape whiteness—that defines them. Morrison has no need of whiteness in her stories at all. Blackness is central to her life, it is entirely authentic, but that's where I part from her.

Neither blackness nor whiteness are central to my life, my aim is to try to write free of it all. The identity writer turns her gaze on me, this time it is the black gaze. How I am supposed to write—what rules am I supposed to follow, what thoughts am I allowed? How black am I supposed to be? These are questions others have faced.

James Baldwin fled America to escape the white gaze and the looks and expectations of his black readers. He was a maverick, he said, a maverick who depended on neither the white world nor the black world. 'I would have been broken otherwise,' he wrote. Going to Europe saved him—as he said, 'it gave me another touchstone—myself'.

In France, Baldwin could be free of identity. The novelist Edmund White wrote:

In France there is no Jewish novel, no black novel, no gay novel; Jews, blacks and gays, of course write about their lives, but they would be offended if they were discussed with regard to religion, ethnicity or gender.

Baldwin said that in going to Paris:

> I wanted to prevent myself from becoming
> merely a Negro; or even merely a Negro
> writer. I wanted to find out in what way
> the specialness of my experiment could
> be made to connect me with other people
> instead of dividing me from them.

Baldwin did not wish to escape being black, but he so desperately wanted to be rid of other people's ideas of blackness. He wanted to write free of the burden of grievance and misery. The protest novel had nothing to offer him, its failure he said, 'lies in its rejection of life'. In France he could look at his country anew, and imagine a time when Americans could forge their own identity 'in the same boat that the American Negro will make peace with himself'.

It is a shame that Baldwin ultimately became what he so detested. He returned to America and swapped the pen for the sword. Conservative black American writer Shelby Steele says, 'Baldwin was transformed in the sixties into an embodiment of black protest.' He advised politicians, he was followed by the FBI, and he palled with Malcolm X, the Black Panthers and Muhammad Ali. Baldwin became the go-to voice of outrage for television news programs, his bug eyes and razor wit became his shtick. Today, to watch those old black-and-white film clips is to be reminded of how compelling he was. But there is a sense of theatre, an absurdity to it all. Baldwin, like the hooded KKK or Bull Connor, the Birmingham Commissioner of Public Safety who turned the hoses and the attack dogs on black protesters, was a different character in the same grotesque American puppet show. Baldwin—for his panache and righteousness—was Punch to America's Judy.

The man who had been raised in the church, who had written so delicately of faith, had forgotten the lessons of his own childhood. He had forgotten about love. He forgot Corinthians 13:4–7: 'Love is patient, love is kind … it does not boast, it is not proud … it is not easily angered … it keeps no record of wrongs.' When Baldwin turned to politics, his words lost no power—perhaps they grew more powerful—but he made the worst bargain I think a writer can make: he swapped freedom for identity and the identity writer can only write propaganda.

America gained the acerbic showman, it got the rapier wit and the raised eyebrow, but it lost James Baldwin the poet. Another African-American writer, Albert Murray, wrote of Baldwin's 'difficulties and confusions as a serious writer'. Murray accused Baldwin of 'laboratory theories of racial oppression' and losing the 'rich, complex, and ambivalent sensibility of the novelist' for the 'thinness' of the polemicist.

I sense that Steele is right: Baldwin's 'fame was out of proportion to his work'. He writes, that Baldwin the protest writer ceases to be a 'mere individual with a mere point of view and becomes, in effect, the embodiment of a moral imperative'. Steele says it is a 'Faustian bargain in which the intellectual knowingly sells his soul to the group.' He says he always thought that Baldwin 'on some level knew that he had lost himself to protest'. Baldwin returned to France and died there in 1987. Steele wonders, did the writer need to be 'out from under the impossible demands of the symbiotically defined black identity, to breathe on his own?'

It is the Baldwin of France that I return to again and again, because he taught me that a black man could have the world. The African-American writing in Paris spoke to a boy living in outback New South Wales and told him that we are not what others insist we are. When I first read *Go Tell It on the Mountain* I understood these black people living with God and race and fear, because they were my people too. And I understood their love because it was the love of my family too. Baldwin spoke to me about many things—anger, righteousness, pain, but above all, love. In France, Baldwin could write of love: love between men, love between white people, love between people, whoever they are.

Let me tell you something else about love: totalitarians hate love; but they love identity. Totalitarians crush love because it is the surest way to crush freedom. People who love too much languish in prisons, they are banished to the gulags or gunned down in the city square. Totalitarians put their mark on those who love, and whom they despise—the scars of the whip, the yellow star on Jewish houses, the burning cross on a lawn, the sign that reads 'no blacks, no dogs, no Irish'.

What a twisted, distorted, mean world we create when we give such power to identity. When the state or the braying crowd determines whether one exists. How much tragedy we have wrought when we put the mark upon people. Where in history have we seen this happen, and where has it not ended in some form of tyranny. Are the lessons of antebellum America, Nazi Germany, Oliver Cromwell's Ireland, Slobodan Milošević's Yugoslavia, Pol Pot's Cambodia, on and on—are they not enough? This is where collective identity, at its worst, can lead: identity that demolishes love.

The truth is—and it is a miserable and shameful thing—that, given a choice between love and survival, most of us choose survival. To survive we will hurriedly betray those who love too much. We become the willing executioners and silent conspirators. We make it easy for the despots—they don't need to control all of us, they just sow fear into one and watch it spread. The Chinese had a saying for this: *sha ji xia hou*, 'kill the chicken to scare the monkey'. In this way Mao built a revolution. Love was a weakness, women loyal to the revolution abandoned their babies in remote villages, leaving them with strangers, so they would not slow the Long March.

What exists in the mind of the totalitarian? What is this desire for unity that breeds tyranny? Theodor Adorno believed he could identify an 'authoritarian personality type'. The German philosopher said it is someone stricken with paranoia and projecting their own aggression onto others. The authoritarian personality seeks to make the world like itself and 'stamps even the familiar as its enemy'. The authoritarian turns unity into totality. Totality: the root of totalitarianism. The totalitarianism of identity that is hell-bent on destruction, that wants to turn time back to year zero. It is the totalitarian identity that destroys the Buddhas of Bamiyan, that sets bombs in theatres and restaurants, that guns down people in prayer.

As a reporter I have seen this so many times. There was a place called slaughter square in a town called Mingora in the Swat

Valley of Pakistan. There, headless corpses were dumped each morning—a warning that a new order was being imposed. A madman who rode a white horse and broadcast bloodthirsty edicts over the FM radio station had seized the town from right under the Pakistani army. He called himself God's messenger and demanded that men grow long beards and women cover themselves and be shut up behind doors. His God— he believed—hated music, hated colourful clothes, hated books.

He proclaimed the will of Allah, but in truth it was his will—the will of the totalitarian. I have met Muslims of extraordinary faith, whose lives are a lesson in humility and generosity. Theirs is a God of love. Now, Mullah Fazlullah made war on their love.

Anyone who transgressed would be publicly whipped, or worse. The 'FM Mullah', as he was known, made sure the world knew about it. He had his own spokesman, a man educated in America who would call me on my mobile phone for interviews.

With the Pakistani military I went into the heart of what was Taliban country in 2009. The army took me and a CNN cameraman into the Mingora town square in heavily fortified jeeps, and wearing flak jackets that may have stopped a bullet in the chest but would have done nothing against a shot between the eyes. They told us we had two minutes on the ground, or then they would leave us behind. Two minutes was all we needed to see the bullet-riddled buildings, the burned-out windows, and the people huddled into the laneways and corners, whatever love was in their lives now replaced with fear.

This is what happens when we banish love, when we no longer see ourselves in each other, but see instead an enemy. The Indian philosopher and economist Amartya Sen has called this 'solitarist identity'. It is, he warned, 'a good way of misunderstanding nearly everyone in the world'. Our shared humanity gets savagely challenged. The solitarist identity has set Hutu against Tutsi in Rwanda, Catholic against Protestant; it is the blood feud between Sunni and Shia Islam, the existential nuclear armed stand-off between India and Pakistan and the partition of 1947 that killed two million Hindus and Muslims and left millions more displaced; the pogrom known as the Night of Broken Glass that set ordinary Germans against Jewish neighbours.

The 'solitarist identity', Sen said, 'can kill—and kill with abandon.'

A lifetime of seeing the worst we can do to each other has often made me wonder if we are not hardwired for hate. If we are not after all that far removed from the law of the jungle. The race hatred of Australia very nearly wrecked the lives of my grandparents. For much of my life, the stories of Keith and Ivy and others like them were held in the 'locked cabinet of Australian history'. But now that we have prised open that lock we are in danger of imposing another tyranny: the tyranny of collective identity.

Our lives are not always sacrificed to the brutality of the world; most of us live with the tender mercies and petty treacheries of the everyday. But it is here that the small wars of identity are fought on local battlefields. Today, after having marked the identifying box, I must go to some or other Indigenous community body to receive a letter of authenticity. Governments tell us this is just an administrative tool, but it is more insidious. What worlds are we creating when we require human beings to be authenticated? We hand power to the Star Chamber that rules on the right of someone to exist. I have seen people broken by rejection, denied the right to decide for themselves who and what they are—denied by the rule of the mob.

I have seen a creeping authoritarian tendency among some people who identify as Indigenous to enforce their view of the world and define their enemies. They wrap themselves in their 'blackness', mocking others and belittling Indigenous people for marrying white. Theirs is an identity of grievance. They see the world through jaundiced eyes and there is a snarling tone in their voice. Theirs is not a righteous anger, but a resentment—an unquenchable thirst for vengeance—that makes them prisoners of the past. They return time and again to that original wound, the source of their identity, and pick away at it so that it forever remains unhealed. I am heartened by the fact that their number is so very few.

I choose another definition for who I am, one not decreed by judges or politicians—it doesn't rely on elaborate word play or forensic blood quantum. It doesn't find common cause with bitterness. It is so simple I can say it in plain English and in one sentence: I will not be anything that does not include my grandmother. I don't wish to be anything that sets me apart from my wife, or any of my ancestors, long lost to history, but whose blood still flows somewhere in me. I will not put a mark in a box that someone has decided contains me. That box that shrinks the endless mystery and possibility of the universe. I will always choose the side of love.

Enough of hate—it has too great a hold on the world already. Enough of the toxic, political imperative of identity—the identity warriors can have that; I am done with it. Identity, even with the best of intentions, falls too easily into the hands of petty tyrants— those identity police who monitor our words and actions, trolling social media to keep people in their lanes, telling us who qualifies to write or read—or monstrous despots who crush love under their boots. Identity carves us up and sets us against each other. There are other words we could use: heritage, ancestry, culture, genetics—words that are far more accurate, words that live in the space between us but do not divide us.

When I think of my life, there are times of great shame. Times when I have let identity harden my heart. I recall coming home fresh from my first year of university, with a vocabulary of new words to show off and a history to lord over people. My mind was full of murder and massacre and disease and theft, and I blamed it on white people—all that they had done to us. I remember telling my uncle whose wife was white how much I hated what these Australians were. He looked at me and said something it has taken me thirty years to fully understand: 'Your aunty would be sorry to hear you say that.'

There have been times in my life I have so wanted to believe in identity. Against all evidence, in spite of all that has been done in its name, I have given it power. As much as I may be tempted by the slogans of 'black pride', 'black is beautiful', yes, even in our time, 'black lives matter'—so urgent, so necessary, so righteous—I stop short. I remind myself that even with the best intentions the solitarist political identity can put us on a slow train to tyranny. I know that tyrants take cover among the righteous. I know now that the identity of empowerment is split from the same atom as the identity of hate. Terror unleashed, crosses all colour lines; remember Rwanda? Identity is the shibboleth of supremacists and sepa-ratists; identity was the secret password that locked the cells of South Africa's Robben Island prison and slammed shut the gates of Auschwitz. Give me instead … love.

My mother wrote about love. This woman born of a black man and a white woman, denied the education she so deserved, wrote poems to love. Never once have I heard her utter the word identity, but she has walked through the world as black, with the love for a black man and black children. Never once has being 'black' meant denying her mother.

She wrote a poem once about broken biscuits—broken biscuits make you cry. Of course it wasn't broken biscuits, it was broken lives. She was writing about the broken lives of her family, her parents, her brothers and sisters, because a country decided for them what they were. A country gave them an identity. It was a poem that took her back to a tin humpy and dirt floors and a gentle, damaged love that kept them alive.

I don't know what word my mother's people the Kamilaroi have for love, but I hope it is like the Greek word: *agape*—the love of God in our hearts. We love because God loves. Here's another secret about love: despots know it will beat them in the end. When they have crushed the identity of the conquered and imposed their own, they know it is only a matter of time before love returns. Napoleon is believed to have said:

> Alexander, Caesar, Charlemagne, and I have built great empires but on what did they depend? They depended on force. But centuries ago Jesus started an empire based on love, and even to this day millions will die for him.

Martin Luther King Jr quoted Napoleon in one of his most famous sermons, 'A Gift of Love'. 'Jesus,' he said, 'is eternally right. History is replete with the bleached bones of nations that refused to listen to him.'

Love is kept alive in the darkest corners and against the greatest of odds. You can put people in chains, you can herd them on boats, you can banish them to faraway lands and love does not die. You can crush people under the boot of oppression, you can gun them down in marketplaces, hang their headless corpses from the town square, and love does not die. People may believe that in identity they will be healed, that in identity there is strength, but in identity there can only difference be—difference where we shut our hearts to love. Identity withers under intense gaze; it is hollow at its core. But love endures when even hope has died.

Aleksandr Solzhenitsyn found love even in the Soviet labour camps. It was the love of humanity in the face of brutality. In *The*

Gulag Archipelago the Russian novelist wrote of his 'First Cell, First Love': 'Of all the cells you've been in, your first cell is a very special one.' He told of how he would remember it all his life, just like a first love. His fellow cell-mates, he said, were his family:

> It was not the dirty floor, nor the murky walls, nor the odour of the latrine bucket that you loved—but those fellow prisoners … and that something that beat between your hearts and theirs.

Solzhenitsyn said that in that cell his soul would heal. That cell became, not an abyss but the most important turning point in his life. His words are majestic. They eschew all hate or revenge; they inspire courage in the most timid soul. In the time of his greatest trial, he pulled humanity closer not pushed it away:

> Now for the first time you were about to see people who were not your enemies. Now for the first time you were about to see others who were alive, who were travelling your road, and whom you could join in yourself with the glorious word 'we'.

In a world where we are putting up more borders and razor wire to keep people out, and identity has become a poisonous new faith, we need these words of Solzhenitsyn more than ever. Solzhenitsyn remembers the sound of the cell door opening for the first time, and 'three unshaven, crumpled pale faces', turning to him and smiling. He had forgotten what a smile was. '"Are you from freedom?" they asked me.'

And there it is. In that one passage from one of the greatest books ever written, we have the answer to toxic identity: freedom and love. All the words in the world and what it is to be human are distilled into just those two: freedom and love. Oh my god, how powerful those words are: freedom and love. Those words have defeated empires. The dream of freedom and the power of love have defied despots. Freedom and love endured the slave ships and could not be crushed under the whip. Freedom and love eventually walked out of Auschwitz and kept alive the memories of those who perished there in those words of defiance: never again.

In my family, freedom and love survived the convict ship from Ireland. Freedom and love burned in the hearts of two people in

1930s Australia—one black, one white—who were driven to the edge by identity that would not see humanity; the politics of identity so brutally put upon Keith and Ivy, my grandparents. I have seen freedom and love in my parents and the life they gave me on the road as a boy—the life of the exile, one step behind and yet in other ways, in the ways of survival, one step ahead of Australia. I am all of that; it is all in me. In that creole garden, there blooms a liberating idea of what it is to be free. In difference we seek identity, yet in difference we are bound to each other—one unrecognisable without the other. As Hegel said, 'identity is difference', 'identity is different from difference'. Ultimately, he wrote, 'identity is in its own self, absolute non-identity'.

Solzhenitsyn, this writer of exile, tells me to embrace the exile in me. The Soviets could not kill what refused to be imprisoned: freedom and love. I read and I write to be free. Indigenous identity is not what I seek—I have that, I don't need to give it a name. I look for my place in the world by tracing the footsteps of all of my ancestors. Yes, I am a Wiradjuri/ Kamilaroi person, I am Irish, I am Australian, I am Indigenous and, as I said before, I have been all of those things and I am none of them. It is exile that calls me on and, yes, some may say that is an identity in itself.

Identity is the new faith—even identity atheists are defined by what they are not. But my identity—if that's what it must be— will not be caged and will not pit me against another. There are privileges in identity that should be called out—the privileges of whiteness, the privileges of masculinity, the privileges of sexuality. These are political questions and, as should be clear by now, I have no desire to be the writer of politics— leave that for someone else—except to say this: we find no liberation behind walls.

There is a question far greater than, 'Are you Aboriginal or Torres Strait Islander? Noongar or Wadjela? Black or white?' It is the question of those prisoners in Solzhenitsyn's cell: 'Are you from freedom?'

Yes.